ZAAGI'IDIWIN:
SILENT, UNQUESTIONABLE
ACT OF LOVE

—

*Leanna Marshall*

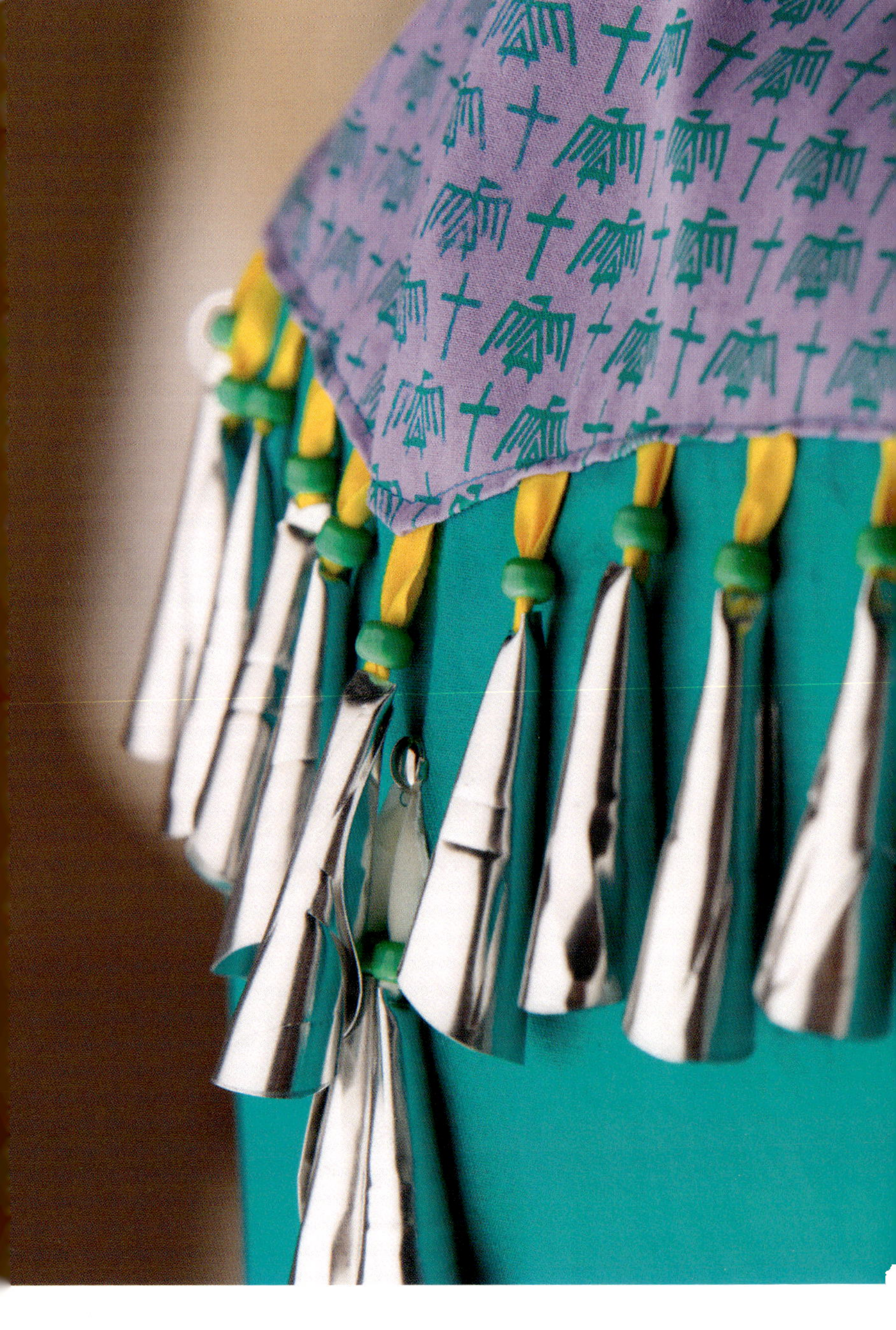

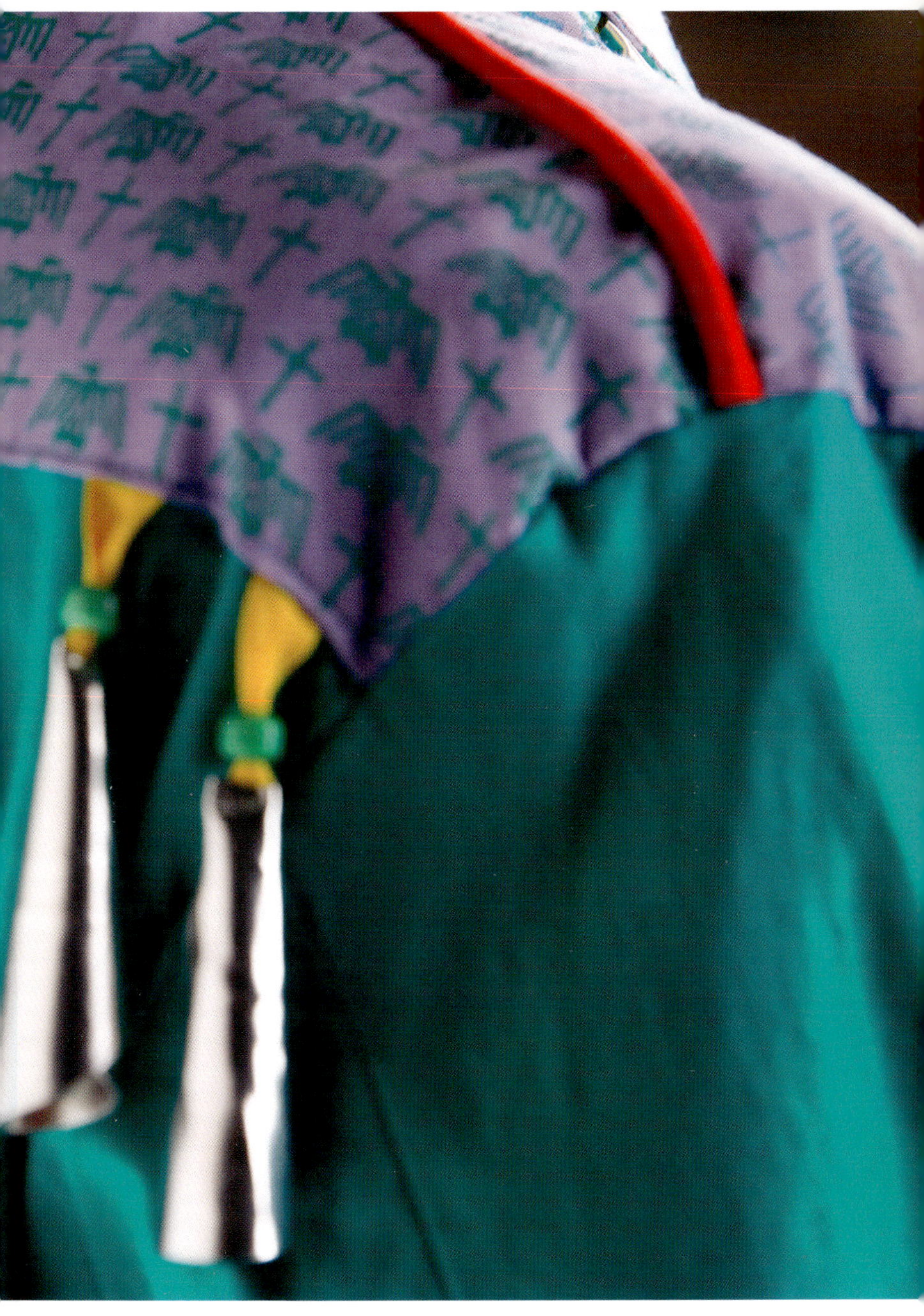

**Treaty #9** (detail), 2016
Broadcloth and homemade jingles
Anemki & cross print by Christian Chapman
Leather, broadcloth, beaver fur moccasins by Jean Marshall

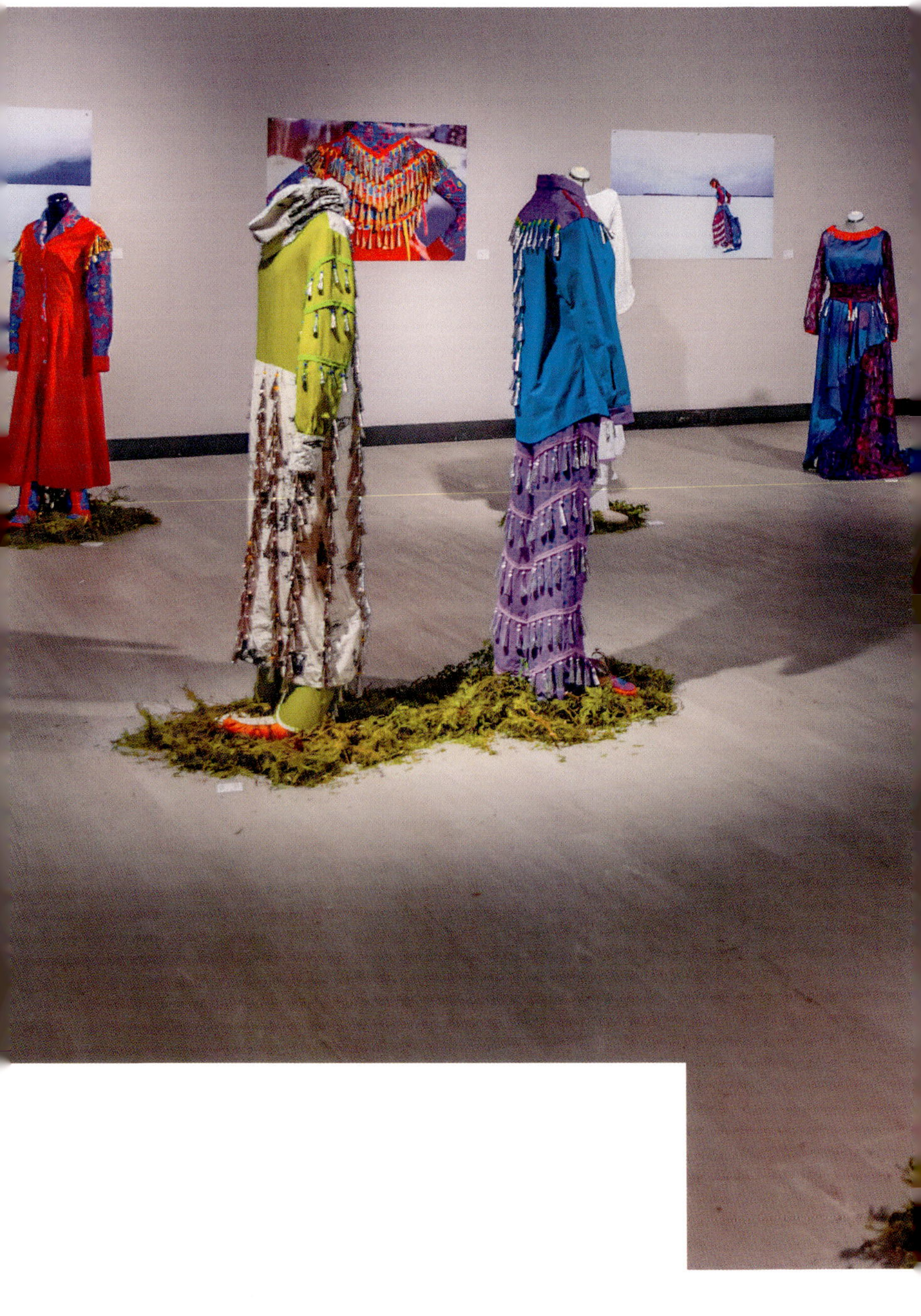

*The meaning of truth is often defined as in accordance with fact or reality. However, how we see truth varies depending on our personal narratives and experiences. The telling of stories provides a framework where understanding, healing, and common ground can emerge.*

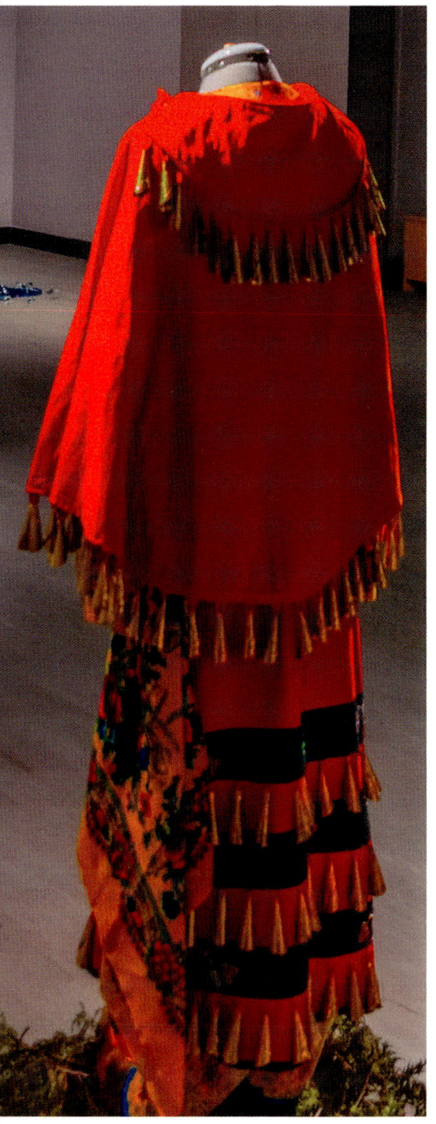

***Zaagi'idiwin: Silent, Unquestionable Act of Love,*** by artist Leanna Marshall creates an intersection where viewers meet to understand and explore the essence of relationships, the meaning of connection/disconnection, and the pain of loss. Through the making and documentation of jingle dresses, Marshall explores the deeply personal stories that have shaped her perception of the complexities of her family history in the context of Canadian history. The social inequities, resistance, and sorrow communicated in this body of work serve as a springboard to examine the act of compassion and forgiveness, which ultimately helps to move forward to a new and more affirmative place of being.

On behalf of the Robert Langen Art Gallery, I would like to sincerely thank Dr. Susan Neylan for her insightful essay that elegantly encapsulates the significance and richness of the art practice of Leanna Marshall. A special thank you to poet Vera Wabegijig for her beautiful prose. To Betty Winge, thank you for your continuous design creativity and dedication to our publications.

Lastly, I extend my deepest gratitude to Leanna Marshall for her open heart, vibrant spirit, and unwavering support in this project. Our journey together on this exhibition and accompanying publication has been a delightful and rewarding experience. For that, I am truly grateful.

The Ontario Arts Council generously supported this publication, and I extend thanks and appreciation for their financial assistance.

*Suzanne Luke*
CURATOR, ROBERT LANGEN ART GALLERY

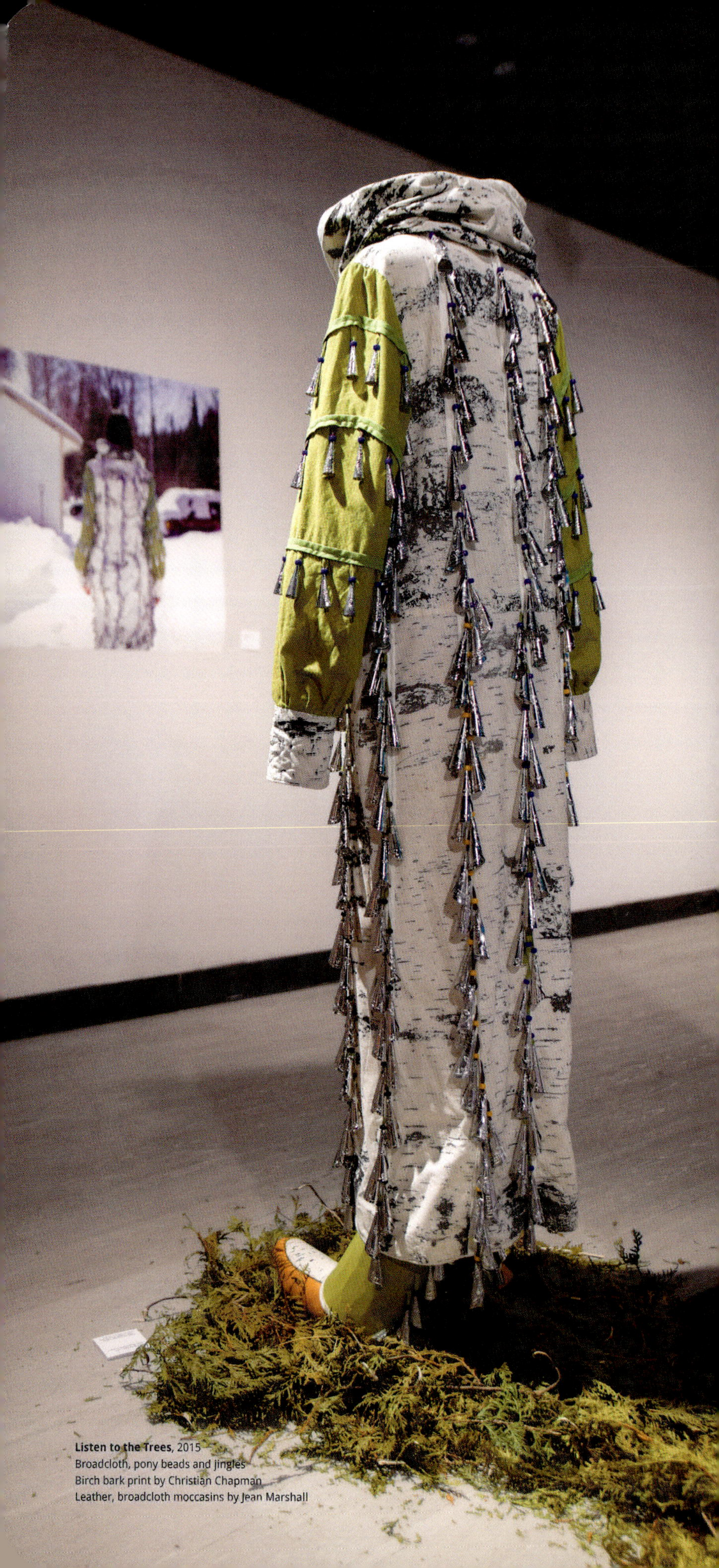


Listen to the Trees, 2015
Broadcloth, pony beads and jingles
Birch bark print by Christian Chapman
Leather, broadcloth moccasins by Jean Marshall

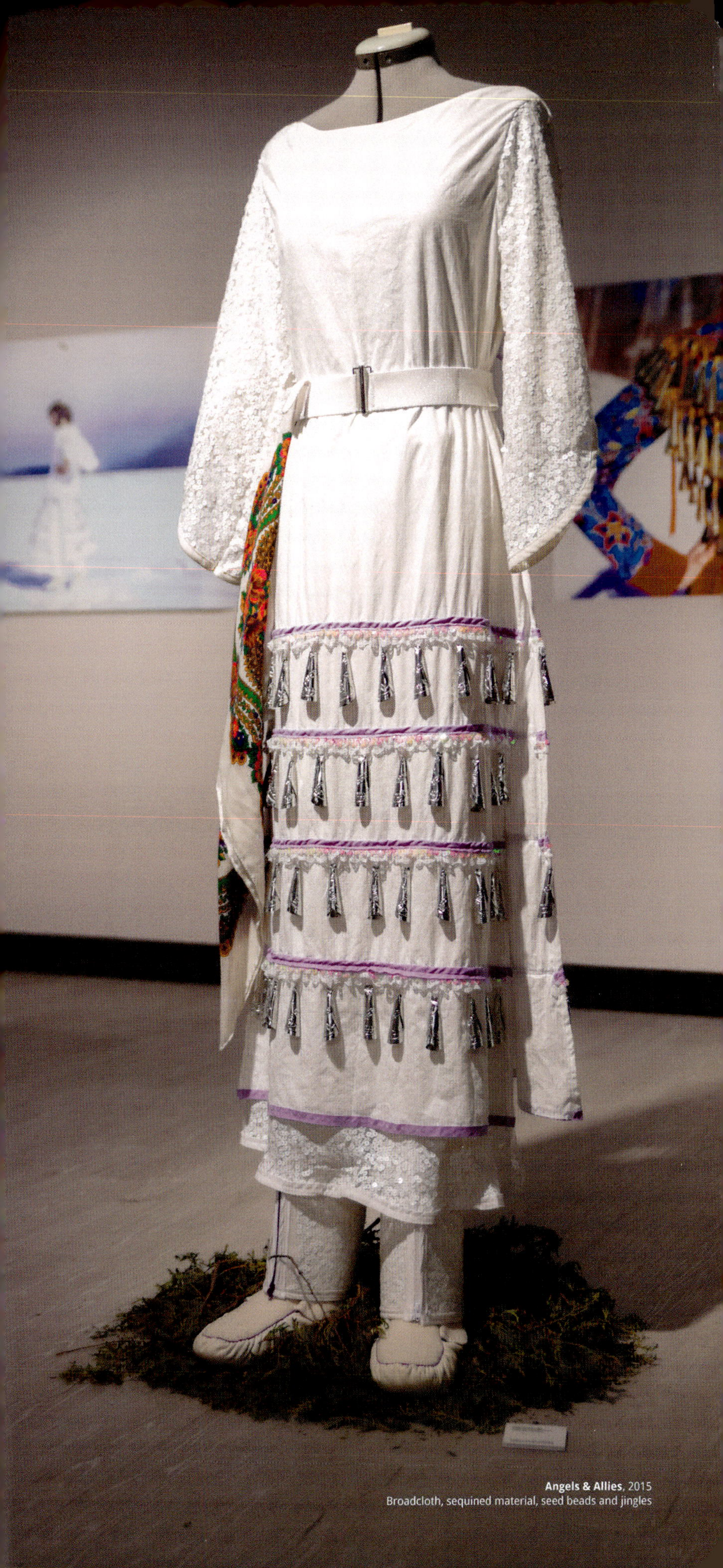

Angels & Allies, 2015
Broadcloth, sequined material, seed beads and jingles

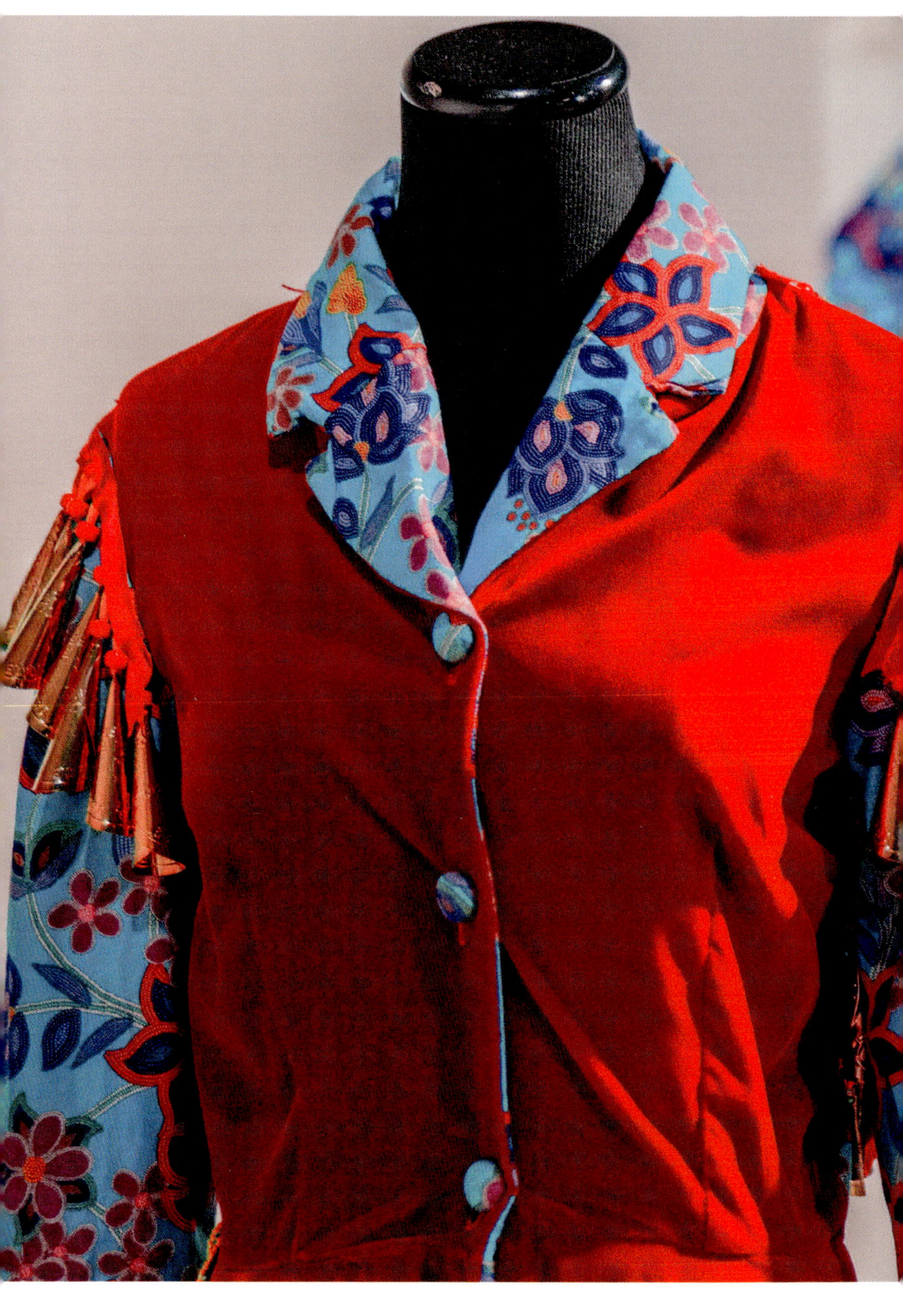

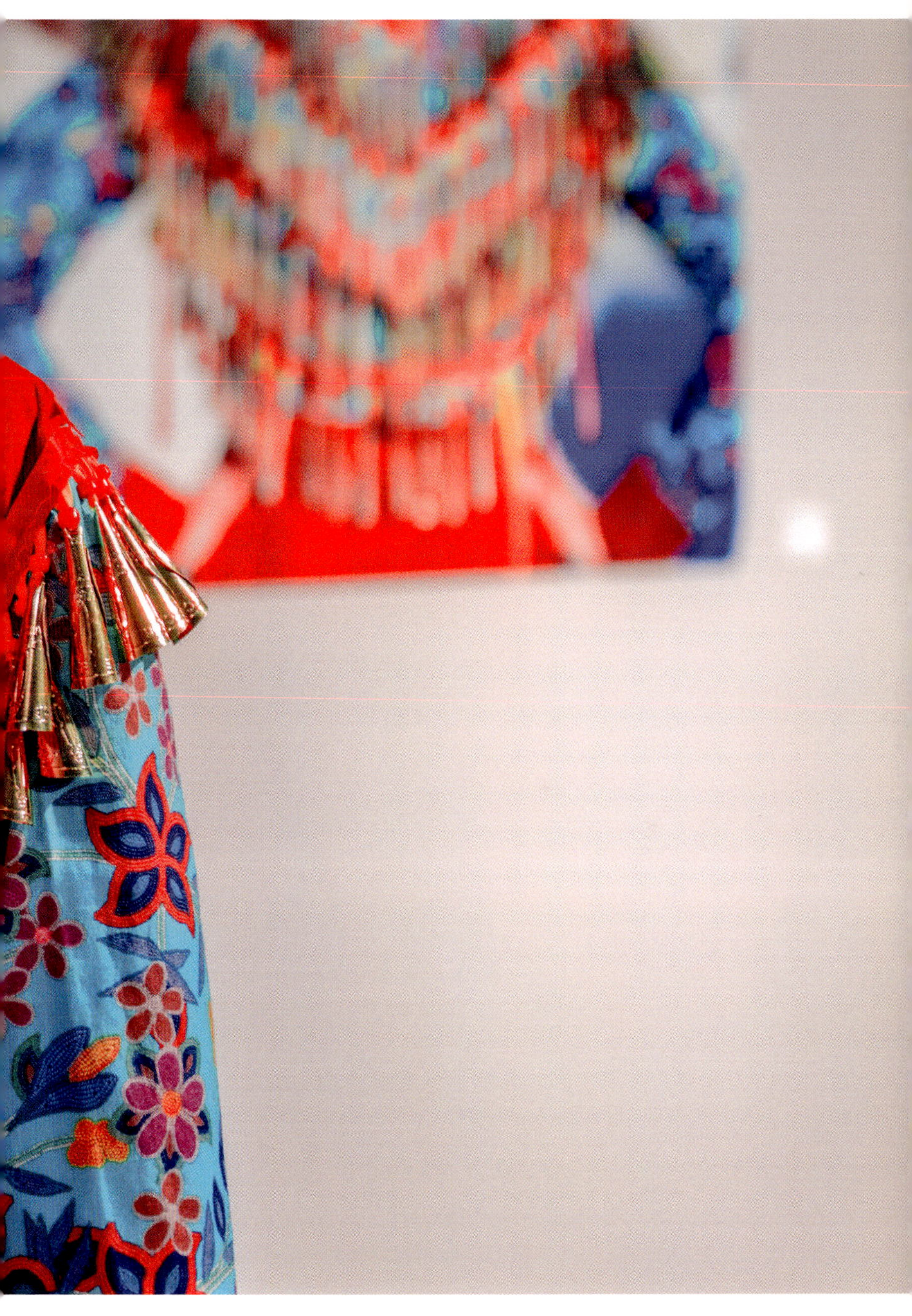

**Give & You Shall Receive** (detail), 2015
Broadcloth, seed beads and copper-coloured jingles

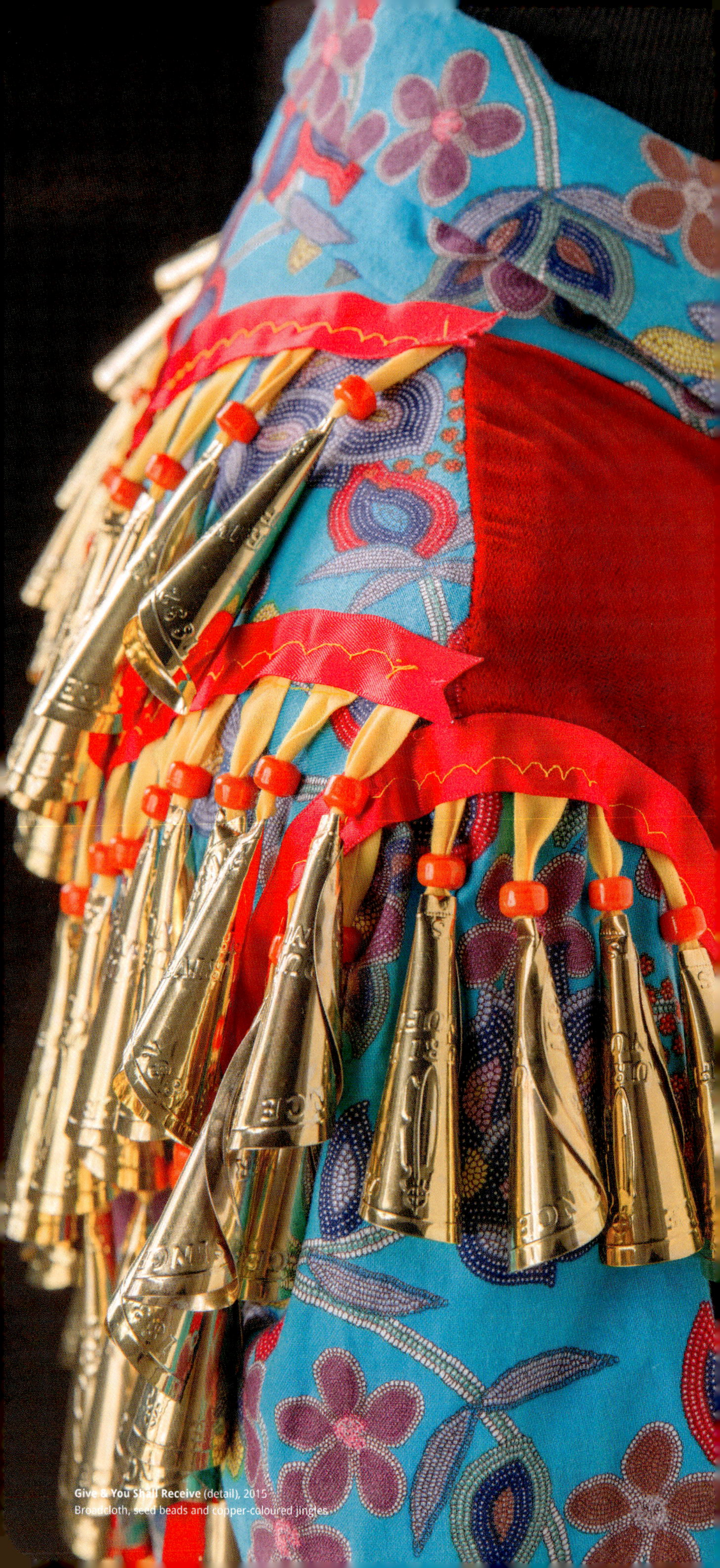


Give & You Shall Receive (detail), 2015
Broadcloth, seed beads and copper-coloured jingles

JINGLES SPEAK
TO THE **HEALING**

—

*by Vera Wabegijig*

*i.*

listen,
ookomis once said,
the longest journey we, humans, will ever take
is the path of healing
it begins when we listen

listen,
mishoomis once said,
the trees connect us through roots
with limbs outstretched, ready to hold, carry us forward
as the mist dissipates with the rising sun
sit, listen
maybe one day you will know
how roots travel into the earth
connecting and grounding
each of us

*ii.*

our voices are vibrations
traveling a path from heart to heart
it is up to us to decipher meaning
like ancestors who had visions seven generations ago
tune into the reverberation

*iii.*

narratives stored in our dna
memories linked to our histories
stories filtered through generations
healing stitched in fabric
hope gathers in jingle dresses

fabric gathers stories along lines of jingles
like tree lines along the shores of  lake superior
with each jingle a story is remembered
like roots running in the earth gathering strength

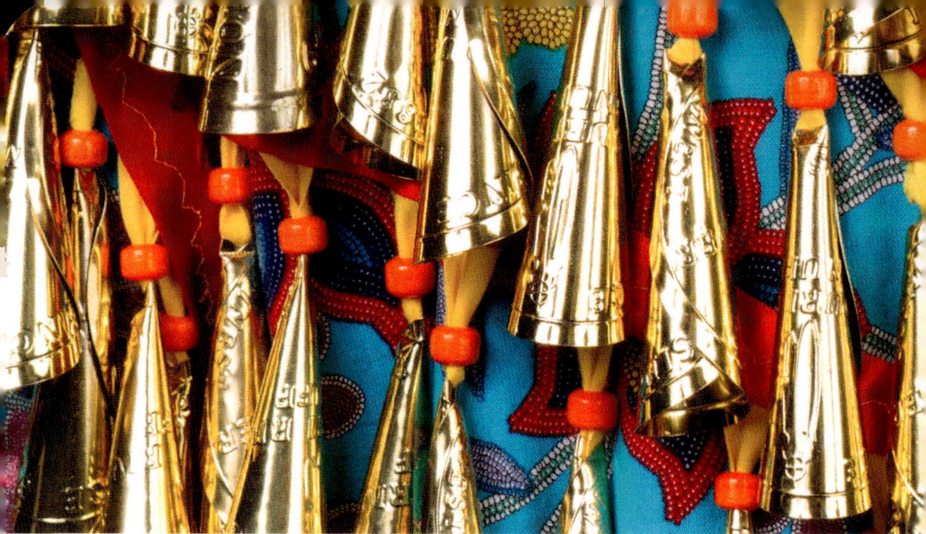

*iv.*

a full moon story
a residual memory
from life at residential school
a painful moon connects broken families

a jingle is placed for each tear
a young girl sheds

a crying moon carries the hurt
as a young girl endures pain from wicked hands

a praying moon enlightens
as a young girl's pain is remembered
with a grandmother's voice

a jingle is stitched for every day at residential school
in each stitch, jingles heal a grandmother's journey
back to a full moon of hope

*v.*

the medicine from the earth
comes through the jingles

jingles speak to the healing
for the women who swim with fishes

each jingle carries a memory
they are not forgotten in each stitch

each jingle carries a prayer
jingles gather along lines of ribbons

the medicine from the water flows
beneath the solid layer of ice

the sound of jingles resonate
frozen in the shuffle steps across lake superior

prayers reverberate below
jingles sound like water and wind as it flows sacred
around you

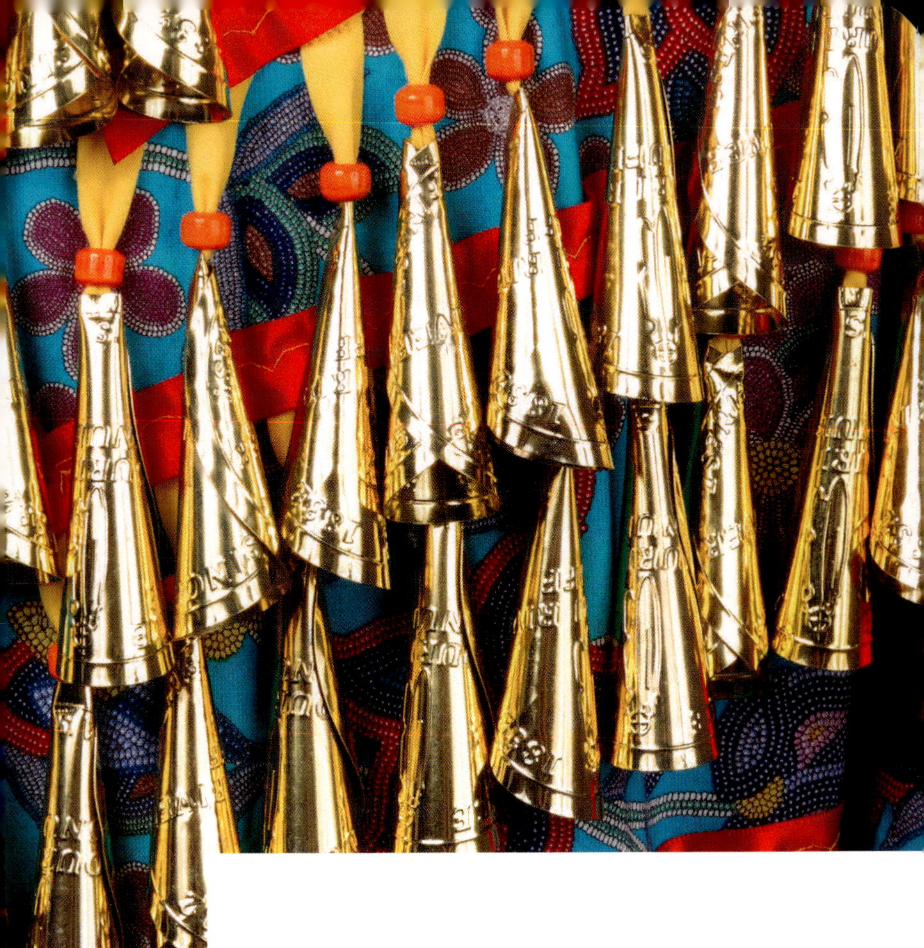

*vi.*

listen to the spirit of the jingle dress

jingle dress dancer
dance with intention

listen to the heart beats coming from the earth

dance for healing
dance for the people who shuffle across the earth

align with the full moon and the cosmos and the ancestors
shake up this world

gather the medicine from the earth
gather the medicine from the water
gather the medicine from the wind
gather the medicine from the trees
gather it all in every jingle

jingle dress dancer
break a new trail and call it a healing path
with each step, jingles ignite the medicine from the earth

healing is constant like the wind
healing is resilient like the land
healing is fluid like the water
healing is sustainable like the trees

these healing dresses
are dancing
listen

*vii.*

listen,
a grandmother once said,
the longest journey we, anishnaabeg, will ever take
is the path of healing and it begins when we listen
with our hearts

the journey from our hearts to our minds
is a path with many obstacles
some we make ourselves
others were there before we were born

there's no short-cut or by-pass
the only way is to find your voice
the voice finds strength with each telling
the chords thread and stitch our lives

remember this and you will honour
voice, story, self

listen,
a grandfather once said,
my story, your story, each of our stories
are important

we carry our stories on our backs
sometimes stories are heavy,
weighing down, curving the spine
like trees bending from the northern wind
sometimes stories are shared
like seeds floating on a summer breeze
taking root wherever they land
becoming medicine from the earth

our stories take root
ground us in the earth
so we can gather the strength
to stand like the trees
and reach for sky

*vii.*

jingle dress dancer
a dreamcatcher
who sees with spirit
zaagi'idiwin guides dreams to those who listen

jingle dress dancer
a collector
who listens with love
zaagi'idiwin travels traplines of history

jingle dress dancer
a seeker
who touches with gentleness
zaagi'idiwin threads through seven generations

jingle dress dancer
a transmitter
who connects to the medicine from the earth
zaagi'idiwin is the teaching in the making

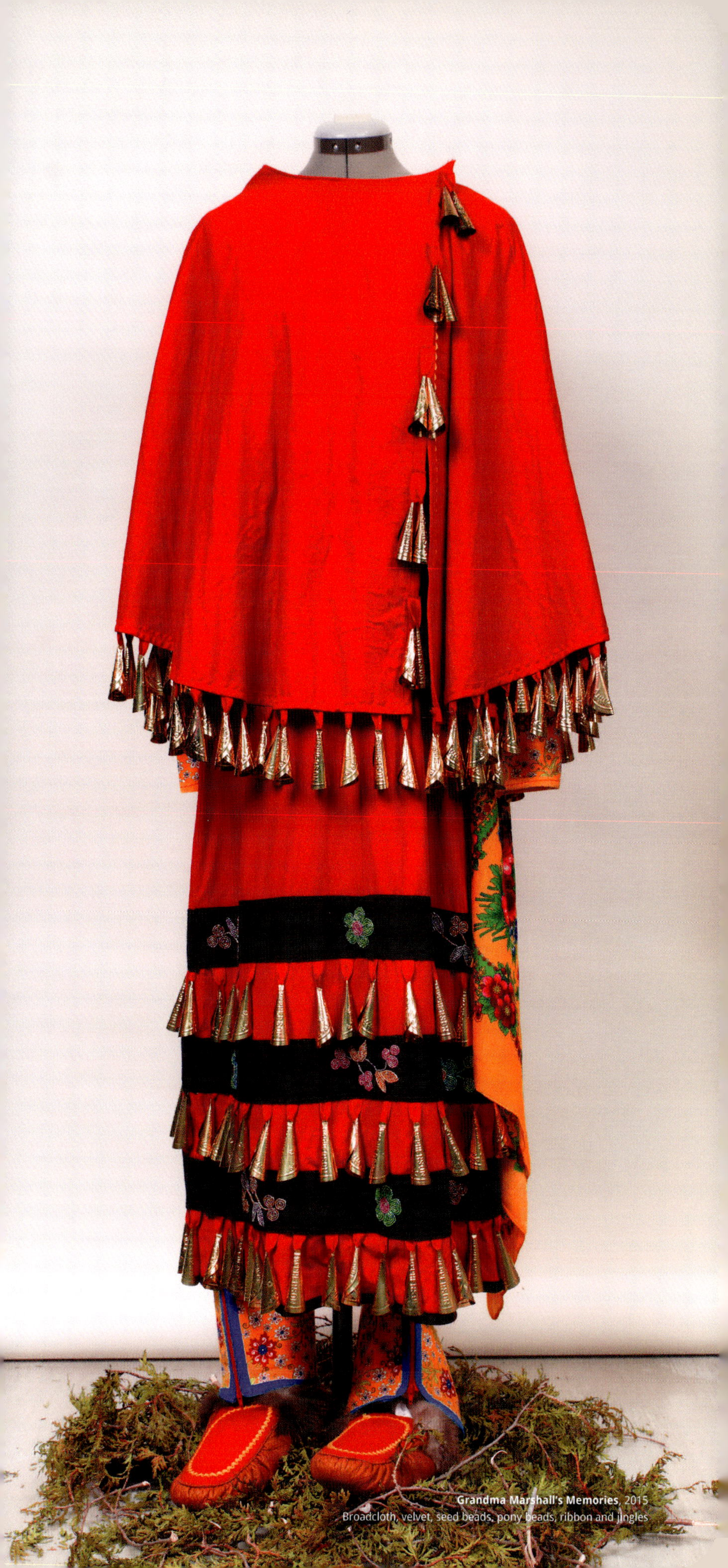

**Grandma Marshall's Memories,** 2015
Broadcloth, velvet, seed beads, pony beads, ribbon and jingles

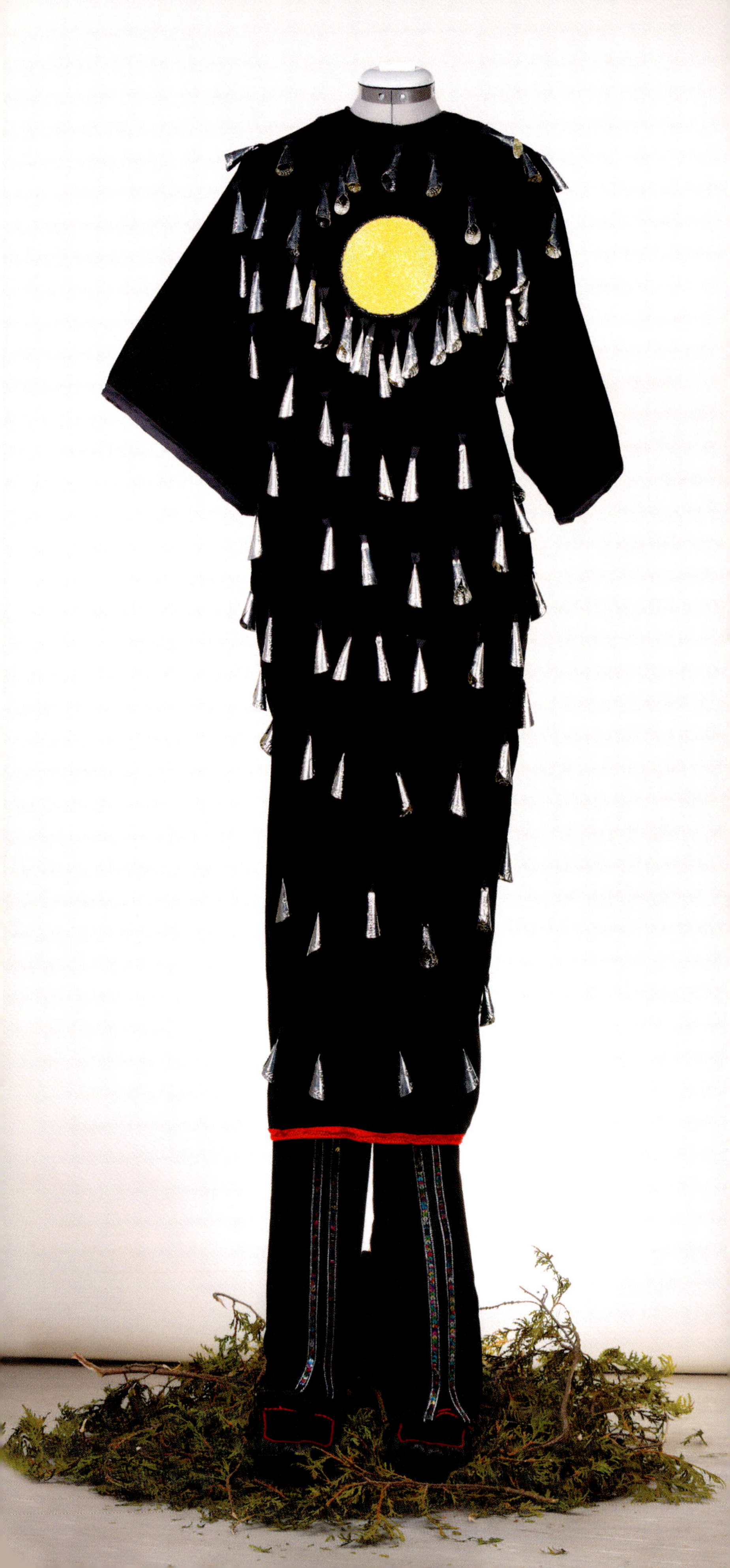

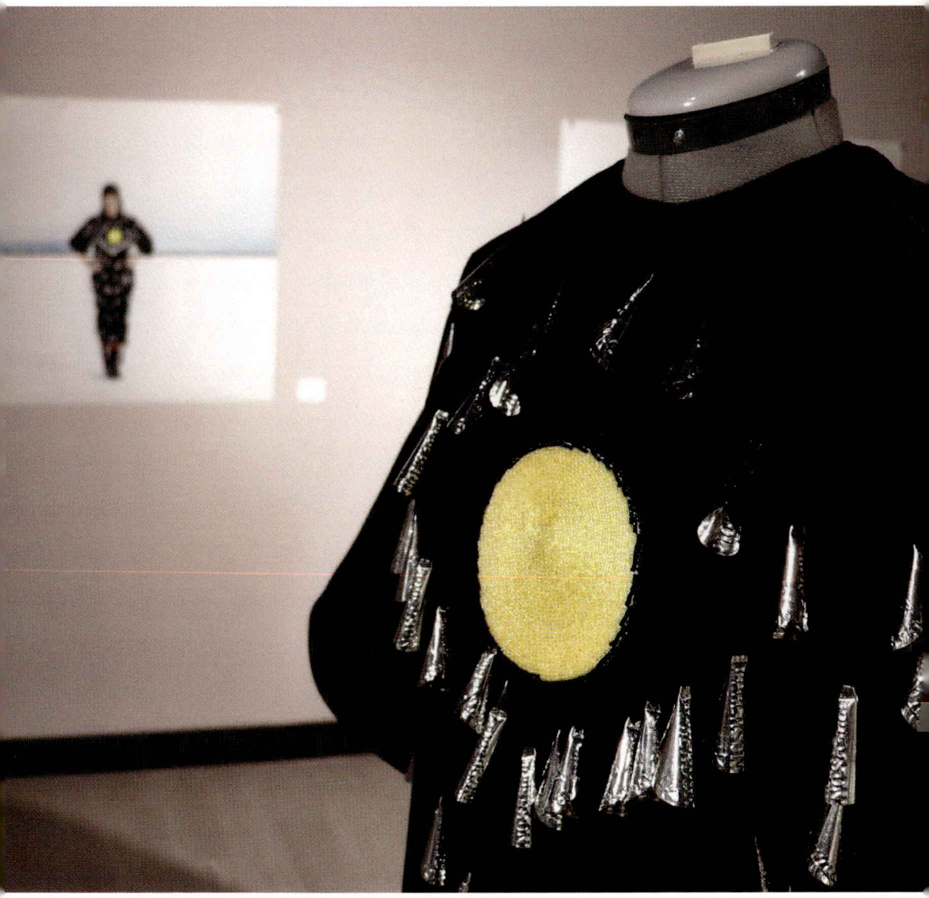

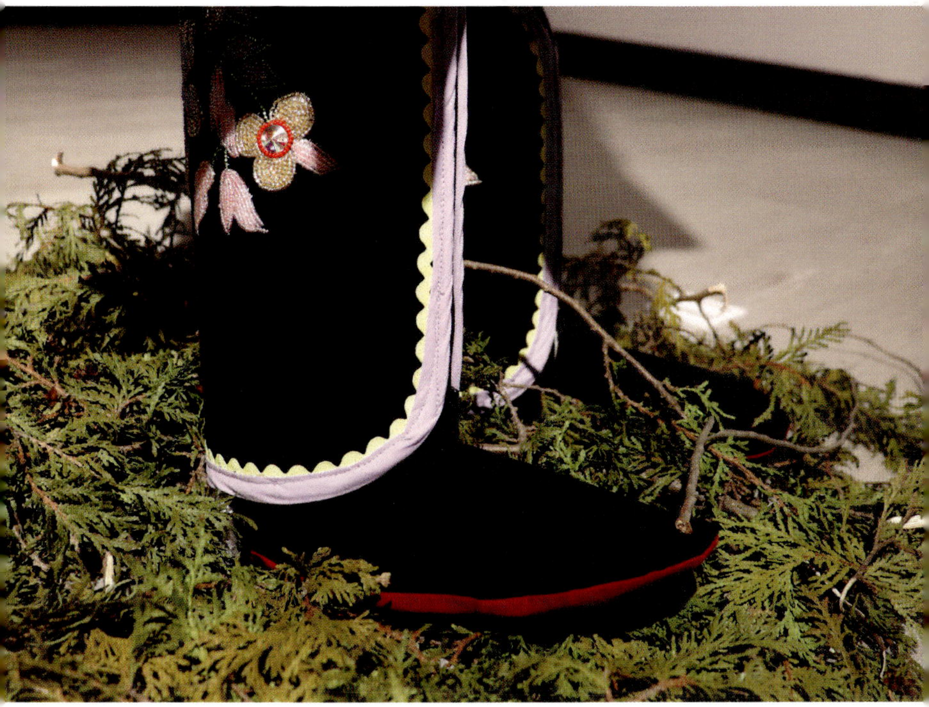

**I Said A Prayer to the Moon**, 2014
Velvet, bias tape and jingles

—

*by Dr. Susan Neylan*

*Art can be powerful and provocative. Through their work, Indigenous artists seek to resist and challenge the cultural understandings of settler-dominated versions of Canada's past and its present reality. Sharing intercultural dialogue about history, responsibility, and transformation through the arts is potentially healing and transformative for both Aboriginal and non-Aboriginal peoples.[1]*

— TRUTH AND RECONCILIATION COMMISSION OF CANADA FINAL REPORT

Leanna Marshall's mixed media installation ***Zaagi'idiwin: Silent, Unquestionable Act of Love*** highlights the power and importance of telling history from personal and cultural vantage points. Indeed, "telling" one's own history, which in the case of Marshall's exhibit, is accomplished through making jingle dresses, becomes itself an act of reconciliation. A member of Kitchenuhmaykoosib Inninuwug currently residing in Thunder Bay, Ontario, Marshall created eight jingle dresses— so called because of the metal cones attached to them which jingle as the wearer moves in them. They are accompanied by photographs of the artist wearing some of the pieces and an audio-loop of her and her mother sharing family stories connected to the dresses. Marshall's jingle

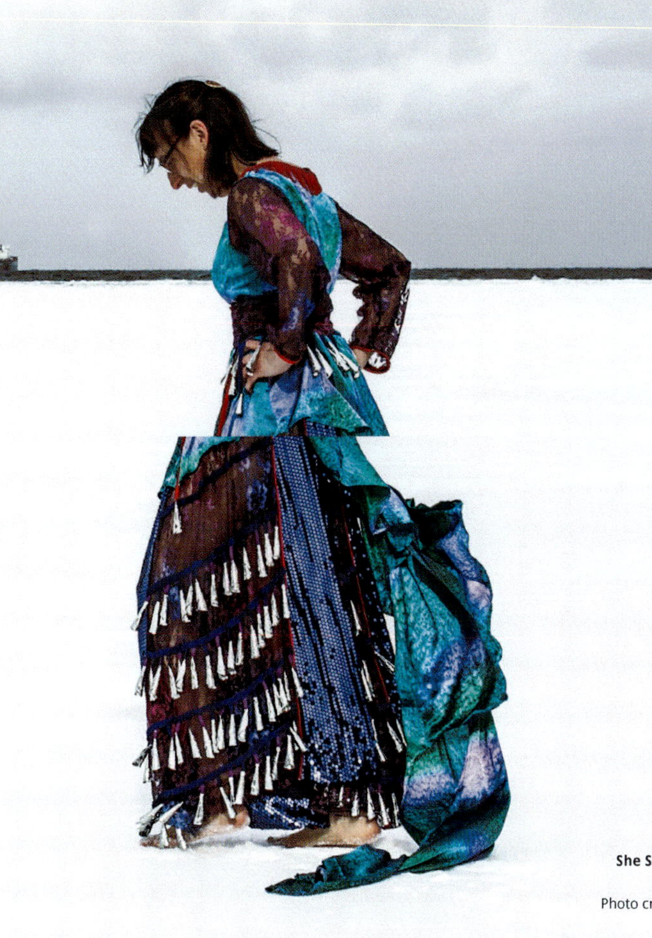

**She Swims with Fishes,** 2016
32"x48", digital print
Photo credit: Nadya Kwandibens

dresses marry Anishinabe traditions and her own artistic innovations. As she explained in her talk at the Robert Langen Gallery on March 8, 2018, jingle dresses are used to extend prayers through dance. "The teachings of the jingle dresses have been an act of love and kindness," for her, she told us; above all, they are healing dresses. She situates them culturally in light of the origins of jingle dresses, for her community at least, with the story of a young sick girl, Maggie White. Maggie's father received the gift of the jingle dress and a song in a dream, and when he let his daughter dance in the dress in the waking world, she was healed. However, Marshall's jingle dresses are also contemporary versions of traditional ones, and through consultation with elders she had been encouraged to adapt them to convey the historical narratives she needed them to convey—for example, making one jingle dress, "Treaty 9," into a set of pants and shirt, to represent a story about her grandfather. Indeed, Marshall calls them "story-dresses," and it is this function that best illustrates how individual creative works and histories grounded in community and family can be effective tools for understanding the history of residential schools and colonialism in Canada.

*[L]ack of historical knowledge has serious consequences for First Nations, Inuit, and Métis peoples, and for Canada as a whole. In government circles, it makes for poor public policy decisions. In the public realm, it reinforces racist attitudes and fuels civic distrust between Aboriginal peoples and other Canadians. Too many Canadians still do not know the history of Aboriginal peoples' contributions to Canada, or understand that by virtue of the historical and modern Treaties negotiated by our government, we are all Treaty people. History plays an important role in reconciliation; to build for the future, Canadians must look to, and learn from, the past.*[2]



In early June 2015, as the Truth and Reconciliation Commission of Canada (TRC) announced its "Calls to Action" recommendations, Commissioner Chief Wilton Littlechild told the gathered audience "Above all, we must remember that this is a Canadian story, not an Indigenous one."[3] Between 2008 and 2015 the TRC documented the history of the "Indian" Residential Schools in this country through the collection of testimonies from survivors, former school staff, and others, and by conducting historical research. The need for really knowing Canada's dark history including all the terrible, genocidal aspects was identified as both a problem to be addressed by listening to voices previously silenced, but also a key element to meaningful reconciliation.[4] But as Canadians how best can we move, as one scholar so aptly expresses it, from a position of collective amnesia, whereby we have denied (or ignored) the history of residential schools and the enduring legacies of Canadian "Indian" policy more broadly, to one of collective reconciliation?[5]

*As the TRC has experienced in every region of the country, creative expression can play a vital role in this national reconciliation, providing alternative voices, vehicles, and venues for expressing historical truths and present hopes. Creative expression supports everyday practices of resistance, healing, and commemoration at individual, community, regional, and national levels.*[6]



One of the thousands of residential school survivors who told their story before the TRC was Leanna Marshall's mother, Charlotte Childforever, whose truth-telling not only had a significant personal impact upon the artist, but it is the very first "story" one encounters in the Zaagi'idiwin exhibit. "I Said a Prayer to the Moon" is a striking black dress with a bright yellow circle positioned over the chest to represent the moon and glittering with jingles from shoulders to hem almost like stars. Marshall's creation embodies the moment when as a child suffering abuse at residential school her mother looked to the moon and prayed for her father to come and take her out of that place. It is heartbreaking, yet encapsulates hope, and it is emotionally impactful. All of Marshall's jingle dresses convey historical moments that connect the viewer with the personal experiences of being Indigenous under colonialism in this country. From the hauntingly beautiful "She Swims with the Fishes," commemorating missing and murdered Indigenous women and girls, or the relationship between Indigenous and Christian spiritualities captured in the motif of Thunderbirds and crosses covering the "Treaty #9" jingle pants, to the "Truth and Reconciliation of Raising Children" dress which situates the disadvantage Indigenous women face in Canada within the context of Marshall's parents' separation and her Indigenous mother's loss of child custody. "We live in a colonial state," Marshall explains, "not one Indigenous woman in this country has not experienced violence. These dresses show one sliver of this history." I think Marshall's exhibit resonates so effectively with audiences, including myself, by privileging not great moments of the past or sweeping generalizations. Rather they show the everyday lives of Marshall's family and her relationships with her kin, making our understanding of history deeper precisely because of that very human, relatable level.

*Collectively Marshall's exhibit helped my history students to consider the ethical and emotional dimensions to historical narration; the jingle dresses moved them to consider similarities and differences between Indigenous and non-Indigenous perspectives on history-telling; and we all came to appreciate the power of personal vantage points when telling the history of Indigenous-Settler relations in Canada.*[7]

*— Dr. Susan Neylan,*
ASSOCIATE PROFESSOR, HISTORY, WILFRID LAURIER UNIVERSITY

———

*Reconciliation of the Indigenous-Settler relationship cannot happen without making the connection between our understanding of the past, a past that often contradicts the dominant narrative of Canada as a kind and benevolent country, and the historical significance of the past in the present. As the TRC Chair, Justice Murray Sinclair, so aptly reminded Canadians, "reconciliation is not an Aboriginal problem — it involves us all."[8] We need to listen to stories that teach us about the dark side of Canadian history, in ways that do not dishearten or shame us, but rather inspire us to enact a process of reconciliation for ourselves. Marshall informed us during her public talk that after the exhibit at the Robert Langen Gallery closes, she will be giving the dresses away, and she'll be moving on to other artistic projects. She reminds us that her pieces are meant to be worn, meant to be danced in, and their jingles meant to heard; her story-dresses will continue their healing and history work yet.*

---


1  Truth and Reconciliation Commission of Canada, *Honouring the Truth, Reconciling for the Future: Final Report of the Truth and Reconciliation Commission of Canada, Volume One: Summary* (Toronto: James Lorimer & Co., 2015), 280.

2  Truth and Reconciliation Commission of Canada, *Honouring the Truth, Reconciling for the Future: Final Report of the Truth and Reconciliation Commission of Canada, Volume One: Summary* (Toronto: James Lorimer & Co., 2015), 8.

3  Chief Wilton Littlechild, *The prepared text of remarks by Justice Murray Sinclair, chair of the Truth and Reconciliation Commission, and Commissioners Marie Wilson and Chief Wilton Littlechild, delivered on 2 June 2015 when the TRC officially presented their 94 recommendations*, 2 June 2015, in "For the Record," Maclean's, http://www.macleans.ca/politics/for-the-record-justice-murray-sinclair-on-residential-schools/,<viewed 25 April 2018>.

4  Truth and Reconciliation Commission of Canada, *Truth and Reconciliation Commission: Calls to Action* (Ottawa: Truth and Reconciliation Commission, 2015), http://www.trc.ca/websites/trcinstitution/File/2015/Findings/Calls_to_Action_English2.pdf,<viewed 25 April 2018>. History education features prominently throughout but especially in Call to Action #62, which states:
We call upon the federal, provincial, and territorial governments, in consultation and collaboration with Survivors, Aboriginal peoples, and educators, to:
    i.   Make age-appropriate curriculum on residential schools, Treaties, and Aboriginal peoples' historical and contemporary contributions to Canada a mandatory education requirement for Kindergarten to Grade Twelve students.
    ii.   Provide the necessary funding to post-secondary institutions to educate teachers on how to integrate Indigenous knowledge and teaching methods into classrooms.
    iii.   Provide the necessary funding to Aboriginal schools to utilize Indigenous knowledge and teaching methods in classrooms.
    iv.   Establish senior-level positions in government at the assistant deputy minister level or higher dedicated to Aboriginal content in education.

5  The phrases collective reconciliation and collective amnesia were taken from Fred Kelly, "Confession of a Born Again Pagan," in *From Truth to Reconciliation: Transforming the Legacy of Residential Schools, eds.* Marlene Brant Castellano, Linda Archibald, and Mike DeGagné, revised edition (Toronto: Aboriginal Healing Foundation, 2011) 29.

6  Truth and Reconciliation Commission of Canada, *Honouring the Truth, Reconciling for the Future: Final Report of the Truth and Reconciliation Commission of Canada, Volume One: Summary* (Toronto: James Lorimer & Co., 2015), 279.

7  Dr. Susan Neylan, instructor, HI345: Native Peoples of Western Canada (Winter 2018). This class was invited to attend the public talk given by Leanna Marshall prior to the opening reception of *Zaagi'idiwin*. One of the assignments in this course was a critical reflection essay based on this exhibit.

8  Justice Murray Sinclair, The *prepared text of remarks by Justice Murray Sinclair, chair of the Truth and Reconciliation Commission, and Commissioners Marie Wilson and Chief Wilton Littlechild, delivered on 2 June 2015 when the TRC officially presented its 94 recommendations*, in "For the Record," Maclean's http://www.macleans.ca/politics/for-the-record-justice-murray-sinclair-on-residential-schools/,<viewed 25 April 2018>.

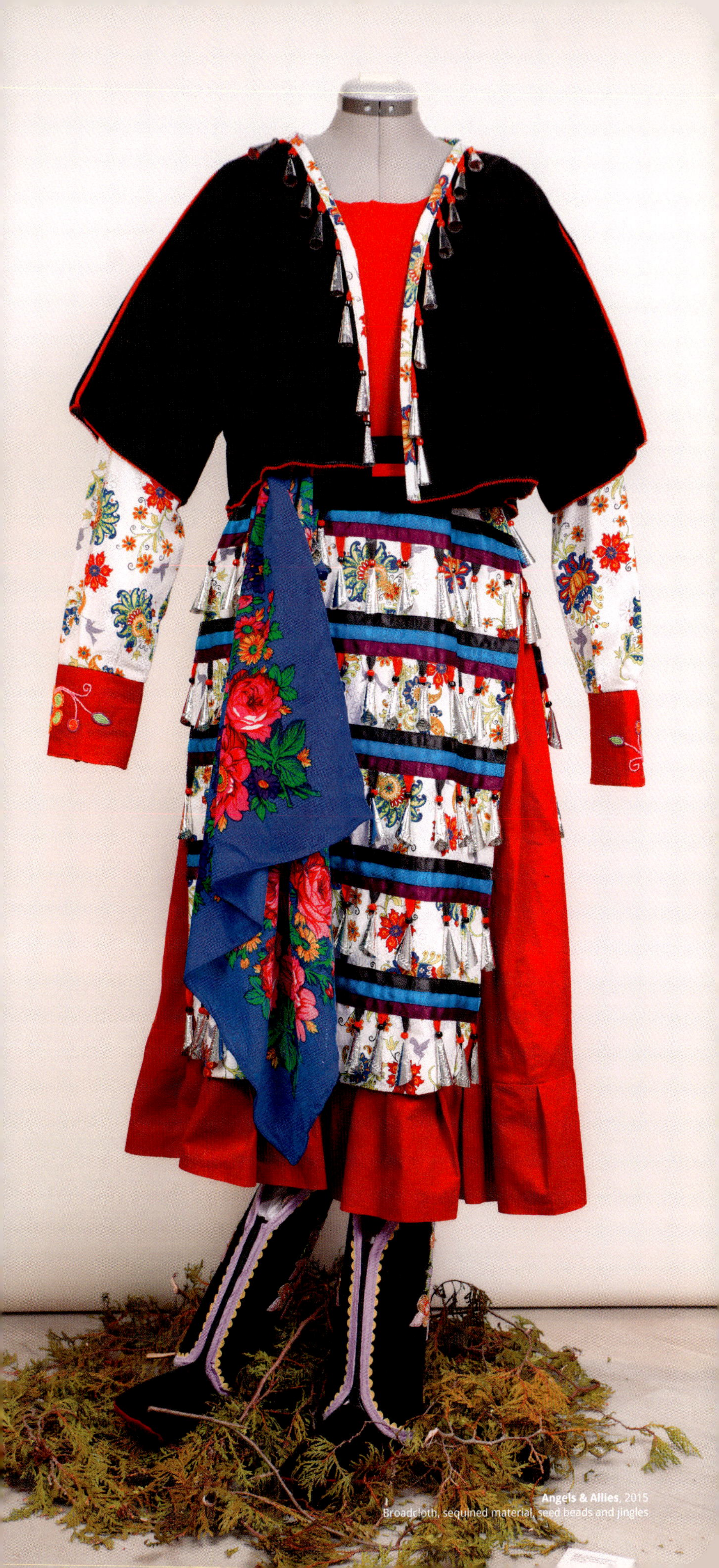

Angels & Allies, 2015
Broadcloth, sequined material, seed beads and jingles

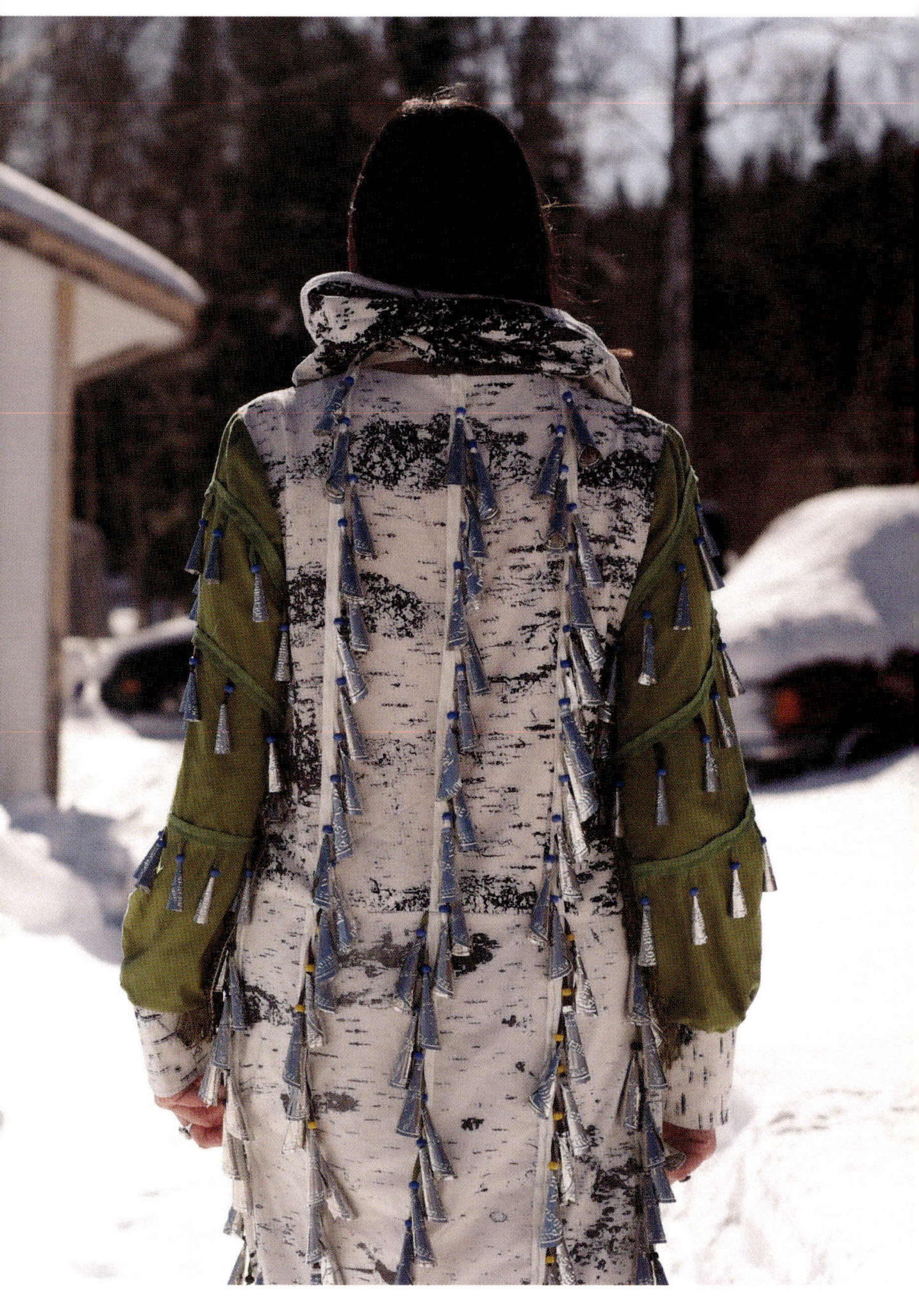

**Listen To The Trees,** 2015
Broadcloth, pony beads and jingles
Birch bark print by Christian Chapman
Leather, broadcloth moccasins by Jean Marshall

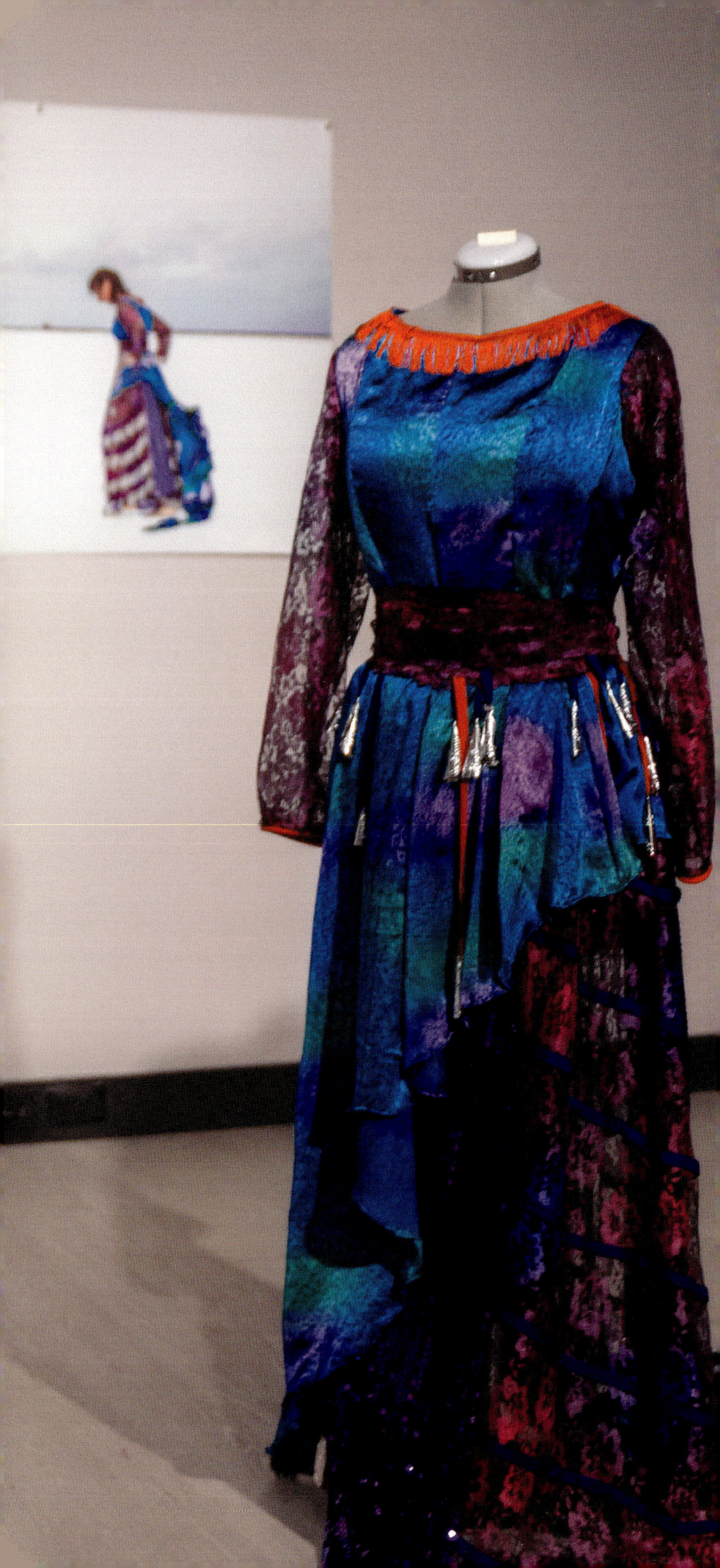

## LEANNA MARSHALL

—

Leanna Marshall is a member of Kitchenuhmaykoosib Inninuwug. She currently lives and resides in Thunder Bay, Ontario. As a maker of jingle dresses and skirts, Leanna tells stories of her ancestors & of the land, and stays in the intersection of where they meet to understand the essence of these relationships: connection, understanding, & healing. As part of the Anemki Art Collective, Leanna was the lead artist in a project called Zaagi'idiwin: Love. She made 8 jingles dresses, each telling a story of her family. The making of these dresses was an act of healing from the oppressive and hurtful history of her family within the colonial context of Canada. These dresses became a part of a group show called The Teaching is in the Making in 2016. This exhibition was shown at the Thunder Bay Art Gallery and the Art Gallery of Sudbury in 2016/17. In addition, this exhibition brought her to speak and perform at the College Art Association (CAA): Crossroads -Indigenous Feminisms in New York City in February 2017. Additionally, Leanna writes poetry and uses performance to express social inequities and to demonstrate actions of compassion. She has contributed a wearable art piece and performance for three consecutive years for the Definitely Superior's annual Derelicte & Urban Infill art events. As well, Leanna is currently involved in the Honouring Our Stories community arts project, which entails working with the Thunder Bay police and women who have experienced sexual violence. Leanna was the keynote speaker for the first Social Justice Conference at Lakehead University in 2017. She created a performance piece entitled: Letter to My Relations which was 4 original letters there were connected by water, resistance, and women. As an act of ceremony, Leanna is wearing skirts for 150 days as we move towards Canada's 150 + years of colonization. Through this she is exploring the space between resistance and acceptance and what the looks like in day to day life, outside of academia and theorizing. Currently, Leanna works as an Indigenous Counsellor at Confederation College where she is also a community activist committed to projects that exploring the deep places of healing from colonial trauma. Along with artists Jean Marshall and Christian Chapman, she is a member of the Anemki Art Collective. Lovingly, Leanna is a mother of two gentle and vibrant daughters.

Robert Langen Art Gallery, 2018
Wilfrid Laurier University
75 University Avenue West
Waterloo, ON  N2L 3C3

Catalogue of an exhibition held at the Robert Langen Art Gallery
February 26 - April 6, 2018

Catalogue Acknowledgements:
*Vera Wabegijig* / LITERARY PIECE
*Dr. Susan Neylan* / ESSAY
*Jordana Garbati* / EDITOR
*Betty Winge* / GRAPHIC DESIGNER
*Waterloo Printing* / PRINTER
*John Ternan* / PHOTOGRAPHER
*Robert Langen Art Gallery* / PUBLISHER

Printed in Canada
ISBN  978-0-9940361-2-4

Zaagi'idiwin was a project by the Anemki Art Collective
and was funded by the OAC-Northern Arts Grant.

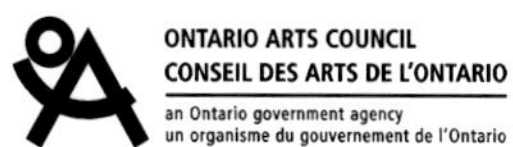


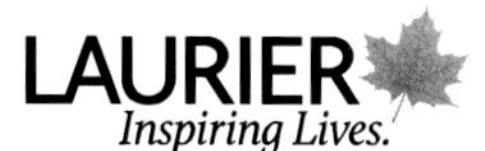